Telehealth for Professionals

What you need to know before logging on

Maryellen Evers LCSW CAADC

2020

First Printing: 2020

ISBN 9781716774911

Maryellen Evers LCSW, CAADC
Dickson City, PA 18719

www.meverslcsw.com

Ordering Information:

Special discounts are available on quantity purchases by corporations, associations, educators, and others. For details, contact the publisher at the above listed address.

U.S. trade bookstores and wholesalers: Please contact Maryellen Evers LCSW, CAADC email meverslcsw@live.com.

Contents

Introduction

In the past, telehealth was used to deal with barriers to treatment such as transportation, child-care, illness, weather, or those living in rural areas. Aside from these situations, many professionals did not see how telehealth could benefit their practice. Most people were resistant and uninterested in offering video conferencing or telehealth sessions to clients.

Once the pandemic overtook our country everybody grabbed their computer systems, ran home, and attempted to continue treatment through a computer or iPad. Most focused on being able to keep servicing our clients. Therapists, doctors, and school systems were ill prepared for the changes which occurred once COVID-19 entered our lives.

The reality is telehealth treatment is *different* from face to face. It is not as simple as merely logging on and having a session. .

Something occurred that many did not expect, using telehealth reduced no show rates and increased counselor productivity . Clients who were familiar with technology were suddenly open and willing to obtain services. Our client numbers did not decrease, as we feared, in most cases they increased.

Telehealth is really a method of service delivery; it is a *modality* of treatment. A method of service delivery that can include individual, group, or family sessions, as well as supervision, visitation, staffing, training or even fidelity monitoring.

There are many different definitions of what telehealth means . In most cases it is dictated by state organizations. To paraphrase, SAMHSA's[1] definition defines telehealth as the use of electronic media and information to provide services. It is used by skilled and knowledgeable professionals. The services are to include screening assessment, primary treatment, and aftercare. It will help people access treatment services and it is used as either a sole treatment modality or in combination with other modalities such as face to face or group.

In this book we will be looking at important facets of telehealth which must be understood prior to performing treatment through this modality.

---

[1] Substance Abuse and Mental Health Services Administration www.SAMHSA.gov

There are specific issues related to telehealth which are completely different from offering face to face service. In a way it is like going from an automatic transmission to a stick shift. While driving is the same…it is different.

These differences are evident within the ethical , legal, and clinical issues of treatment. "Telehealth for Professionals- What you need to know before logging on" offers knowledge related specifically to those areas, as well as providing insight into the use of technology with adolescents and information related to the ever-changing world of technology. This book will offer you concise information related to each of these areas that cannot be ignored when providing telehealth services. Offering telehealth services really is more than just logging on.

Ethics

Ethics, quite frankly, was one of the most challenging courses in my graduate education. I cannot recall anybody who would kick their heels heading into ethics class; but it is a foundation of our profession. It is our responsibility as professionals to maintain ethical standards of care with the clients we treat.

Ethics is the discipline dealing with what is good and bad and with moral duty and obligation. One of the primary ethical considerations we must take, when offering the modality of treatment, is assessing appropriateness. Not every competent clinician is a good candidate for telehealth, and not every client with a computer should be a telehealth client.

When looking at the clinician we must assess if our foundation of clinical skills is strong. We must consider our own experience and knowledge related to the clinical skills we possess. Clinicians will be called upon to use skills and information not typically asked for when offering face to face services. A major challenge in providing ethical telehealth is the lack of supervision available. The use of this modality is so new to our field that finding a professional who has knowledge, skills, and experience to "supervise" others is like finding a needle in a haystack.

Ethically, it is in our best interest to have a frank conversation with the clients we work with even before the clinical assessment begins. It is important to speak with them about their thoughts and

feelings related to treatment via a computer. A client's motivation for treatment through technology
usually dictates their engagement in their treatment.
Be sure your client can maintain their safety as well
as the safety of others while participating in telehealth treatment. This conversation needs to not
only include questions regarding their internet access but also their computer equipment. Offering
telehealth to those with limited internet access or
poor computer capability will lead to multiple issues
within the telehealth session. Those limits could affect the overall treatment for the client. Any
technological limits will also prove frustrating for
you as the clinician.

An ongoing ethical debate related to telehealth is the question is telehealth ethical or is

denying online services unethical? While ethics always consists of those grey areas that are open for debate, what we need to do professionally is to learn the limits and uses of technology and the modality of telehealth as opposed to simply stating it is an unethical modality of treatment.

Ethics in telehealth is not a new topic. George Stricker, former head of the APA Ethics Committee, discussed "Psychotherapy in cyberspace"[2] in 1996. Even back then issues such as the therapeutic relationship and responsibility, identity of the client, emergency contact, privacy of online communication, and dispute resolutions were discussed. An approved set of guidelines for ethical practice of telemedicine was finally created. In these

---

[2] Stricker, G. (1996). Psychotherapy in cyberspace. *Ethics & Behavior, 6*(2), 169, 175–177.

guidelines it states, "chief among these guidelines is a directive that the clinician understands that technology does not trump medical ethics." This brings us to the ethical dilemma of just because I can do it, should I?

An ethical code of conduct was created in 1999 by health care law and mental health professionals to offer a set of ethical standards for health care organizations. The "high ethics alliance" (health internet ethics alliance} was made up of several online health providers such as WebMD. This alliance created a consensus in 2000 on a code of ethics for the medical "E health sector". While these guidelines were initially created with medical providers in mind, their ethical standards were applicable to mental health and substance abuse treatment.

In 2009 Janaki Santhiveeran PhD reviewed the compliance of social workers online therapy to the NASW code of ethics standards.[3] He found that less than half of the sites studied, 44%, provided information to clients about how to safeguard their privacy while engaging in the online mental health services. Barely half, 49%, provided statements about the duty to maintain confidentiality. Only 1/3, 32%, included specific emergency protocols beyond

---

[3] Compliance of Social Work E-therapy Websites to the NASW Code of Ethics Janaki Santhiveeran PhD
Pages 1-13 | Received 19 Sep 2007, Accepted 25 Apr 2008, Published online: 02 Jan 2009.

the mere reference to 911. Providing ethical tele-health treatment to any client that we work with is our professional responsibility. We, as profession-als, need to be sure we increase the compliance compared to those in 2009.

To help you with specific guidelines for your professional practice online I have narrowed down the top 10 ethical considerations you should con-sider when implementing in your telehealth practice.[4]

1. It is our ethical responsibility when working online to educate ourselves about the uses and limits of online care. It is further our responsibility to advise our potential clients about

---

[4] EthicsCode.com: "Guidelines for Mental Health Practice Online."

those limits. It is also ethically important that online practitioners inform potential clients of any relevant research and available data about online therapy including the potential effectiveness or limits to a specific diagnosis.

2. Online clinicians assess the suitability of potential clients for online care. Online care may be insufficient for clients in crisis or life-threatening situations where in person assessment and care is a better alternative. If we as an online practitioner foresee that a potential client may require in office care at some point, it is our

ethical responsibility to inform the client of such. The clinician accepts the client into care only if both parties agree that the therapist is within a reasonable geographical distance of the client and can thus provide in office care if needed or a contingency referral arrangement for such cases is mutually agreed upon by the clinician and the client.

3. Online clinicians must verify that the client's identity is truly the client. While that may seem out of the norm, keep in mind we may be working with mandated clients. If Jim

must do 20 hours of therapy for pro-

bation how do we know he is not

paying his brother $20 a session to

sit there and pretend to be him ? As

clinicians we need to find ways to

verify the identity of our clients

through some other established

means aside from face to face inter-

action. Some ideas which may aid in

this practice could include clients

holding up a driver's license or state

ID into the camera at the start of an

assessment. Another idea would be to

not only have the client offer their

Social Security number but also a

code word that was sent to them via email prior to the session.

4. Verifying identity also comes into play when obtaining emergency contact information from our clients. I always remind folks when teaching not to assume the emergency contact placed on intake paperwork is going to be your client's emergency contact during telehealth services. Keep in mind , if Joe is at his office for therapy, and his wife is on the paperwork as his emergency contact, his wife will not be with him during his session time. It is imperative that clients

not only identify an emergency contact who will be nearby when they
attend their telehealth session; but,
also that all releases of information
are signed. This allows you, as the
clinician, to reach out to the identified person without fear of breaking
confidentiality

5. Understand your limits of license and
insurance. During the COVID-19
pandemic many waivers and exclu-
sions were offered. Parity compacts
were signed between states. State licensing boards loosened various
restrictions. It is not uncommon for

one person to be sitting in New Jersey while their therapist is in Pennsylvania. It is our responsibility as clinicians to provide professional care only to those clients who reside in the state in which we as practitioners are licensed or certified. Online clinicians must explain the limits of these out-of-state practice laws and consider how it will further affect the client's insurance coverage. I have had to discharge a client because they moved from Pennsylvania to New York and I did not hold a NY social work license, my limits of licensure

prevented me from continuing to
treat them.

6. It is our ethical responsibility to educate ourselves and advise clients of
the potential risks to confidentiality
regarding therapy via the internet.
Not only do we have to consider our
own physical environment, and
where we are performing our services, but it is our responsibility to
educate our client on ways to keep
therapeutic sessions as private as possible. We cannot offer 100%
confidentiality when technology is
used. While there are multiple layers
of security, we can put in place such

as passwords, secondary authentica-

tion, virtual private networks and

encrypted programs, there is always

going to be a risk that information

sent over the Internet may be com-

promised. While the federal and

state reactions to the COVID-19 pan-

demic eased the rules and regulations

required for privacy, it is of the ut-

most importance that we as clinicians

provide care only through secure

websites using current protective pro-

cedures. Realistically speaking apps

such as FaceTime or Google hangout

are not HIPAA compliant forms of

communication. While free or low-priced video conferencing platforms seem attractive, you must be sure that it follows HIPAA and is sent over an encrypted Internet connection.

7. Another ethical responsibility we have as providers includes advising our clients of the limits of online care as it relates to payments or reimbursement with third party providers. We cannot assume that insurance companies, whether it be federal, state, or private pay funded will automatically cover telehealth sessions. It is up to us to offer due diligence and stay educated about payments

and reimbursement requirements for online professional services.

8. When offering online services, we must also keep in mind regulating and supervising entities. Online providers are responsible for providing links to information of bodies that license, certify or supervise us and to whom clients have recourse in case a dispute arises. Just as our agencies often have posters hanging in waiting rooms or entrances, we must virtually hang this information. For many this information is incorporated into their telehealth informed consent or posted on their website.

9. No matter your licensing body, professional standards must be adhered to. These professional standards include the privacy of client records. Office procedures inclusive of detailed descriptions are required and kept in a non-virtual office. Here the question becomes how you secure information on your laptop. Securing information is not just a matter of having a password protected computer. These professional standards include securing downloaded information obtained by clients on our

computers, electronical medical records, assessments, progress notes,
and correspondence.

10. As telehealth clinicians our primary
ethical responsibility is to master this
modality of treatment. We must seek
out technical consultation or other
means of understanding technical issues prior to providing online
professional services . In some cases,
this may mean practicing at home
with the Internet platform you will be
providing services through. It could
also mean peer support groups, or
even reaching out to those have who

have been offering telehealth treatment for a substantial amount of time and pay for supervision.

Professionals engaging in telehealth therapy must follow all requirements of their professions code of ethics. It is our responsibility to assess not only the client for appropriateness, but we need to assess our own skills and abilities. As with any licensed professional we are only to offer services within the scope of our practice. Keeping this in mind, if one is not trained in telehealth, one should not provide it.

Let us say you log into your telehealth session and your client is sitting there with a cigarette. Are you comfortable with your clients smoking or would you direct them to put it out? Ethically what is the appropriate way to hand this? You log on to your session and discover your client is drinking a beer? Is it ethical to allow your client to have an alcoholic beverage during your treatment session? Finally, what if you are logging off your telehealth session only to discover you did not completely disconnect. You suddenly hear your client and their partner in possibly a domestic violence incident. What would you do?

These are just examples of how telehealth is different from face to face. So, while we will say telehealth is the same as face to face but different, knowing how to handle situations in an ethical manner is an important foundation in providing telehealth treatment.

Legal

It is important for us as clinicians to gain the knowledge of jurisdictional issues as well as understand the need for a secure environment when practicing telehealth. Telehealth guidelines vary from state to state. What is most important is that you follow up with not just your state laws but also your specific licensing board. Please know, I am NOT an attorney. The information I share is based on my knowledge and experience and it should not be construed as legal advice. If you need legal information regarding your agency or practice, please consult with your agency or personal attorney.

The laws regarding confidentiality are extremely important issues to understand when providing telehealth. The Health Insurance Portability and Accountability Act (HIPAA) has been in place to protect client health insurance information since 1996. In accordance with HIPAA compliance it is essential that you use a platform that will offer a secure virtual environment. Currently there are many companies offering these services. While I personally use ZOOM, there are others such as Doxyme and Microsoft Teams. While I do not endorse or support any specific platform, what is most important to know is that the platform you use should be encrypted, secure, and offer a business associate agreement. A business associate agreement, or "BAA", is an agreement between you, as the clinician, and the platform provider. The easiest way to explain a BAA is that your platform provider ensures no information will be saved. Along with a HIPAA compliant platform, it is imperative that you also use a HIPAA compliant email server. These secure email services , such as the compliant platforms, offer encryption at both ends. Simply using a Hotmail account or AOL account will not provide you the level of safety and security needed for your professional work.

If you provide drug and alcohol treatment and are a federally funded program, you must also comply with 42 CFR Part 2. The core values of 42 CFR Part 2 include promoting treatment, reducing stigma, confidentiality, and nurturing the doctor client relationship. With limited exceptions, 42 CFR Part 2 requires a client's consent for disclosures and these disclosures must be in writing. Releases and documentation can be signed electronically. Programs such as "Digisign", "Docusign" or "Adobe" provide this service. Another option would be to have your client take a picture of their signed Informed Consent and e-mail it to. When all else fails there is still snail-mail. Please be aware that "verbal consent" is not allowed under 42 CFR Part 2. Often, we will document "Pt. gave verbal consent blah blah blah…" Do not sell yourself short and leave yourself open for legal or confidentiality issues. Having policies and procedures in place in how to obtain client signatures while offering virtual therapy is something which must be considered when preparing to offer telehealth.

Confidentiality means I cannot tell anyone what I know . Anonymity means I do not know. HIPAA falls under the concept of "I cannot tell anyone what I know". 42 CFR Part 2 falls under the "I do not know anything" category. Using the "best practices" and "most restrictive standards" as you create your telehealth practice will only benefit you when "waivers" and "exceptions" are retracted from various funding sources.

Legally, one of the most frequent questions I get asked is regarding the informed consent. I offer you an example of one in the resources section. You certainly do not have to recreate the wheel as many templates are now available. The informed consent for telehealth that you use must contain the following:

1. Nature of treatment

2. The risks

3. The benefits

4. Alternatives to treatment

5. An opportunity for client questions.

I also incorporate the client's emergency contact information into my informed consent as well as the name of the platform I use for sessions and a specific policy regarding social media.

In addition to the HIPAA compliant platform, emails, and informed consent, there are other legal issues to be consider. One would be to include questions related to your client's online life within the assessment. This could become a legal issue if a client has what is referred to as a "second life" they may present information that could otherwise be re-portable. For example, I once had a 20- something year old enter his session extremely excited about who he killed. While my clinical brain was reeling about appropriate steps I am mandated to take, I was 5 minutes into the session when I realized this client was discussing an avatar he uses in a combative game. His "reality" is one in which his online life is a source of pride and excitement. Knowing his online history would have aided me a few moments of concern.

Your liability insurance is something that cannot be overlooked either. While most malprac-tice insurance carriers now include coverage of telehealth services, you must be sure your policy does. If you live in a state where you can provide services across state lines you need to review your policy as well. Some insurance companies will only cover you for services practiced in the state you reside. We must also look at fee structure as well as truth in advertising. Many agency websites will place an advertisement banner stating, "now offering telehealth". It is our legal and professional responsibility to identify those clinicians who have been trained to provide this service to the clients we offer services to.

I previously noted I include a social media clause in my telehealth consent. A reality of telehealth is that a strange dual relationship is created between the client and the clinician. This cyber relationship is different compared to the relationship we build with our face to face clients. Clients who use telehealth become more comfortable emailing, texting, or reaching out to you via social media. It is not uncommon that your client will Google you prior to calling. Any personal information you have on the internet, social media sites, political affiliations or local newspapers is easily accessible and available for clients to read. I suggest you "Google" your own name so you can become aware of what your clients are seeing about you in cyberspace.

Our clients often do not understand a power differential could occur clinically if they discover personal information about us. Keep in mind while some social media sites allow you to "accept" friendships or followers, other social media sites simply allow people to follow you. Discussing these boundaries and expectations with you client while reviewing the informed consent will help in preventing any misunderstandings during treatment.

One final thought in the legal and jurisdictional application of telehealth is related to reimbursement and funder issues. Federal, state, and private pay funders all have their own requirements. "Waivers" were offered during the COVID-19 pandemic allowing treatment in otherwise unacceptable modalities such as telephonically. I suggest to all who offered telehealth as a reaction to the pandemic to create a program which is compliant with legal and ethical standards of pre-COVID treatment, not states of emergency. It is up to us to perform due diligence when submitting information to insurances , CPT codes, reimbursement, and copays. Information is changing quickly and frequently from

these organizations. Professionally we are expected
to stay up to date with all changes. A useful organi-
zation to help keep you up to date regarding legal
issues is the Office of Excellence in Protected
Health Information. A list of other organizations is
provided for you in the Resources section as well.

Clinical

Clinical principles and standards of conduct-ing a telehealth session are an essential skill in order to provide the best clinical care possible. Currently there is no overseeing body that offers "certifica-tion" in telehealth. One of the reasons this is not an option is because a certification requires role play-ing, supervision, and testing. While there are companies who will offer a "certificate" in tele-health, many are overpriced, and no licensing body requires certification to perform this modality of treatment.

There are differences in counseling tech-niques between face to face and telehealth sessions. Not only do we need to be sure it fits the client, clin-ical preparation for a telehealth session is quite different than a face to face session. Prior to the clinical work even beginning it is important to work with the client on understanding what expectations are when moving from face to face to telehealth treatment sessions. There is a set of "online ground rules" when offering telehealth. These "online ground rules" are important to review with your client when discussing various treatment modalities. As noted, once technology is used for treatment there seems to be a shift in how frequently a client may reach out to you via text, email, or private message. It is important to specifically explain the boundaries of telehealth treatment to your clients.

There is a different type of "front end" work when doing telehealth as compared to face to face sessions. It is important to prepare, as to make the clients experience as safe and clinically sound as it can be. I need to be responsible for preparing my own environment prior to the telehealth session. I want to "model" professionalism to my client. When working from home I alert my household members that I am heading into a session, I hang a "Do Not Disturb" sign, secure my pets, quiet my own distractions, and grab the emergency information cards for those I am seeing during the day. Preparing in this manner saves valuable time if I need to address any emergencies during a client's session.

I prepare for my sessions differently now too. No longer do I sit and wait for my clients to show up at my office. I "invite" them to their session now via email. I email my clients a link to their session every morning. While some programs offer a continuous "web office", others change the "room" you will be using for the session. To enhance the safety and confidentiality of our sessions I choose to change the "room" we meet in each time. This is a personal choice of mine, and while it does create more "front end" work for me, it does enhance the privacy of my sessions.

When using telehealth, I also put more thought into where I anticipate my session may go. When in the office I can easily reach into my file cabinet to offer a handout for my client to read. When providing telehealth treatment, I must have the documents I think I may be using ready to share. I have a file on my computer desktop called "File Cabinet". In here I have my most frequently used documents. I will not lose session time scurrying about my computer to find a document I want to share in a session. I simply go to my "virtual file cabinet" and pull them out prior to the start of the session. Keep in mind, if you are sharing your computer screen without preparation, you are increasing the risk of sharing not only your personal information but also potentially one of your other clients. Even the "bookmarks" we have in our browser will be visible. Adjust your settings to prevent any inadvertent disclosure of your personal information. Close your unused programs, disconnect from any messaging programs and be sure your electronic medical record is not able to be viewed. Look at your own computer desktop – are there any documents or forms you would not want your client to see?

There will be situations you should prepare for during telehealth sessions that you will not have to think about when doing face to face. Whether it be a child screaming in the background, a partner walking into the room in the middle of the session, or a screen that suddenly goes blank due to technology issues. Be prepared on how to handle these situations because they will happen. There have been times I have logged into a session only to find my male client merely wearing boxer shorts or the client who logged in while pushing a cart in a store thinking it was "OK" to have our session while they were shopping. Put thought into how you will ad-

dress these "unexpected" situations which we do not

have to deal with when working from our office.

Another major difference when using tele-

health is that at a click of a button your client can

leave a session. Years ago, I worked in an adoles-

cent residential treatment facility. During a family

session the adolescent became upset and stormed

out of my office. I was able to keep an eye on them

from a distance. I could observe their body language

, and their behaviors. I was able to de-escalate him

prior to re-engaging them back into the session.

These steps that I took to work with my client in that

situation will not be useful in telehealth. This is the

primary reason it is importance to have a safety

checklist or safety plan. Knowing the patients physical address during the session, emergency contact information, and having steps you will take if the client ends the session abruptly is essential for client safety. Being prepared is the most important facet of telehealth because the client is not within the walls of our office. Not only could they easily end a session in an abrupt manner, but there could also be increased verbalizations of negativity or increase distractions. It is important to know how to handle these situations to keep the client safe and their clinical progress moving in the right direction.

Reviewing the session check-in sheet at the beginning of each session is a way client safety is monitored. An example of a session a check in sheet is provided for you in the resource section. Check the physical location of where the client is at the time of the session, check their technology, safety, and confidentiality. Having a viable phone number that we can communicate with them as well as their emergency contact person information will expedite help if needed.

Another useful tool to use during telehealth sessions is that of a safe word. A safe word is useful in that if the client is interrupted during the session, they could say the identified word to alert the clinician to mute and disengage the video. I work with my client on identifying a safe word they are comfortable with. Often, we will use the safe word "coffee". If I am working with a client and their significant other walks in interrupting our session the client could simply say "hold on I need a cup of coffee" or "hey is that a coffee?". That alerts me to the breach of my client's confidentiality, safety, or comfort in our session.

Just because your client may be a 20 something year old who loves technology , it does not mean that they are appropriate for telehealth. There are several diagnoses you may not feel comfortable with working via a telehealth modality. Some clients deemed inappropriate for telehealth could be those with extensive suicidal or homicidal ideations or attempts, thought disorder diagnosis, or those not stabilized with their medication. Personally speaking, I will not treat those addicted to pornography or gaming via telehealth primarily because the computer is the tool they use to feed their addiction.

Determining if a patient is appropriate for telehealth treatment is a personal choice. Keep in mind however, you are liable for the treatment you provide.

Up to this point, clinically, we have not even begun working with our client. The "front-end" preparations and safety planning are activities we put into motion even before we dive into the interactive part of our therapy session. Once we finally do start working with our client via telehealth, a wonderful starting point is to explore and discover your client's online life , technology experience, and comfort level. This is more than asking "are you comfortable with online sessions". This is an actual assessment of your client's online life.

There are many unmonitored group chats, websites, self-help forums, and Facebook groups where inappropriate, or even dangerous information may be shared. Asking our clients about their participation in these types of online communities allows us to better understand their point of view or frame of reference as they enter telehealth treatment.

Using telehealth as a treatment modality requires different therapeutic skills. It is a balance of not only clinical skills but technological skills. It is knowing enough technology to aid your client when issues arise with their Internet access, computer, or platform. We as clinicians also use a different communication style when using telehealth. Reflective listening and feedback are used more frequently as to verify the clinician's understanding of the client's verbalizations.

I find myself using more descriptive words as well – more adjectives. For example, as opposed to the open ended statement of "tell me more about feeling overwhelmed" I phrase it as "I hear your overwhelmed, are you feeling like you are carrying a rock or that you are trudging in neck deep water?"

I have often heard from students "I am not a fan of telehealth; how do you build empathy or observe body language if you can only see them from the neck up?". Here in lies the benefit of participating in a multi-week, experiential, online course about telehealth. This amazing thing occurs for my students a few weeks in. Relationships are built. Feelings are expressed and shared. Empathy, sympathy, and support are demonstrated. All the reservations therapists had regarding relationship building are debunked. Simply completing a CEU on telehealth, or even reading this book, will not demonstrate this to you. I can attest to it though, not only as a trainer and educator but also a clinician.

Our clinical skills shift when performing tel-etherapy. We learn to pick up on nuances we may not have otherwise seen in face to face sessions. While I may note a client's foot tapping while in front of me in my office, I notice their fingers being rubbed together during the telehealth session. Our auditory and visual senses are amplified. I have a client with a long history of trauma. During our telehealth sessions, when he becomes anxious or un-comfortable, I can hear him playing with a drawer. You may hear a client's ring tapping against their coffee cup. These sounds alert me to an emotional shift.

Pets can also be a tool to aid in assessing a client's emotional state. At times, pets are used as a distraction or tool for avoidance during telehealth sessions. I have several clients who, once becoming uncomfortable, will attempt to divert the topic by placing their pet in the computer. Others may use their pet as a tool for comfort and place the animal in their lap and pet the animal during our session.

Remember, we do not just sit in front of a camera and observe. We drive the bus. I may ask a client "Can you tell me what is going on your body right now?" or "May I ask what you are doing with your hands/feet as we talk about this?'. Again, while there are some similarities with the dynamics of an in-office session, this is where telehealth is different.

One of the most challenging clinical services being provided via telehealth is that of group therapy. While the same legal, ethical, and clinical issues apply, there are other elements which need to be considered. Many agencies are finding it useful to have peers or para-professionals call group members the day prior to verify their safety checklist data. Best practice in providing group is to have co-facilitators running group. One, performing the lead clinical work while the other handles any technical, behavioral, or safety issues in the background. It is also best to have either an "in person" or "on-line" group. Offering a "hybrid" or "In and Out" type of group setting creates an "inner" and "outer" group dynamic which will affect the clinical progress and outcome for group members. Another challenge is the length of time groups are held for, especially in the Intensive Outpatient Program's. Consider offering a 10-minute break after every 50 minutes of group time. The shorter, more frequent, breaks will aid not just your client's but also yourself.

Eventually updated rules and regulations will fall into place regarding the use of telehealth as a treatment modality. Telehealth treatment will not be limited to those only living in rural areas or with transportation problems. Those with physical mobility issues, scheduling conflicts, parents working from home or caretakers of the elderly will be able to obtain treatment services more easily. Even as this material is being put together for publication, private pay insurances, as well as federal and state agencies are looking at the limits, they imposed on telehealth prior to COVID-19. Rest assure, research is being conducted and while waivers will be re-tracted, the acceptance of telehealth as a viable treatment modality will be incorporated into payor source policies.

Adolescent

Just as we would work with different populations in our offices you may be called upon to work with these different populations in your provision of telehealth. Clinically we certainly do not work with our middle age adults in the same manner we would work with a 15-year-old adolescent.

We know technology has changed the face of adolescence. In my day we did not have the cell phones , laptops, or computers. We did not have "portals" or "hubs" to check in with our teachers or to check our grades. Those of up growing up during or prior the 70's are termed "digital immigrants". Those who grew up playing on smart phones, tablets, and computers; are considered "digital natives".

We keep this in mind as we know serving an adolescent population brings up different clinical issues. Not only do we know the psychological and physiological differences in teenagers, but we must also keep in mind there are technology differences as well.

When working with this population of clients it is important to ask ourselves how familiar are we with technology and the internet? I will admit many an adolescent client has taught me a thing or two when it comes to social media and computer apps. When working with this populations it is more than just knowing the latest technological trend.

The Pew Research center conducted a survey in 2018 entitled "Teens, social media, and technology 2018".[5] This data demonstrates close to 95% of adolescence either have or have access to a smart phone. This is a 22% increase from the same research which was completed in 2014/2015.[6] We can clearly see adolescence have the world at their fingertips.

When comparing the 2014/ 2015 data to the 2018 data there is a stark difference in the percentage of teenagers who claimed to be "constantly online". While 24% of respondents identified being

[5] Pew Research Center, May 2018, "Teens, Social Media & Technology 2018"
[6] Pew Research Center, April 2015, "Teens, Social Media & Technology Overview 2015"

continually online in the first survey, 45% of adoles-

cence identified continual use a mere three years

later when the same question was asked.

Think back to the clinical section of this

book when I shared the importance of knowing your

client's online life and how this information can be

useful and easily obtained in an assessment. Talking

with the adolescent or child you treat regarding the

programs and platforms they use will enlighten you

to their peer groups, influences, and friends. Issues

such as bullying, catfishing, and self-trolling are

important online behaviors which today's adoles-

cents face.

The use of technology and the internet for to-

day's adolescence has even altered definitions.

Today's adolescences have a different definition for

what they consider a "friend". The definition of a

friend when I was a teenager was one who I would

hang out with after school, or on the weekends.

They lived in my town and we would meet up on

our bikes and go to the town park. Our days were

spent in the summer swimming at the town pool or

romping through the woods. Today's youth identify

"friends" as those they have connected with through

technology but have never physically met. Adoles-

cent may appear more open and comfortable during

telehealth sessions as compared to face to face ses-

sions. For the "digital native" communicating

through technological devices seems second nature.

Keep in mind though, technology is so natural for

this younger generation that they often have a diffi-

cult time discerning between a social connection via

technology compared to therapy. We often have to educate the adolescent client to appropriate boundaries and expectations within telehealth services.

Not only is the role of technology and the internet for an adolescent one aspect which makes treating them different via telehealth, there are other considerations you must be mindful of. When using telehealth, you must put thought into how you will obtain input from the adolescence family members. Youth often have differential diagnosis which may be slightly more challenging to work with through telehealth as well.

Safety is the most important things to consider. When working with adolescents it is not only their safety we have to prepare for. We must be mindful of the safety of those who will be with them during their telehealth session. You must assess if the caretaker could ground or diffuse the youth if oppositional behaviors or upset occur during the telehealth session. When we work with adolescents or children via telehealth, we must also include their caregiver in not only safety planning but in the use of interventions.

Just because you are 13-year-old client can sign on by themselves and log into your telehealth session, will it be safe for them to do this with no parent or adult figure in the house? How will you clinically handle any disclosures of self-harm or self-mutilation the client may share? In face to face sessions, we often include the caregiver at some point in the session. The adolescent will return to the waiting room while the parent comes into the office.

You must ask yourself how this will look in a tele-health session? Will the child leave the computer and go into another room while the parent speaks to you? Will you have the parent log on to the session from a different location in the home? How will you clinically handle privacy if a parent refuses to allow a child a safe space to talk to you by frequently in-terrupting or eavesdropping? Knowing how you will handle these situations will prepare you for providing therapy with your adolescent client's and their families.

Another aspect to consider when working with adolescent or children is your own style of therapy. Do you offer play therapy? Is there suffi-cient room for your client to draw or color? How will you have them share their drawing with you?

How can you incorporate sand tray therapy through online telehealth sessions? How about the use of games and learning tools within a therapy session? Do not be afraid to move your camera around or have your client move theirs. Encourage the adolescent to discuss their surroundings with you and share information related to what you see in the background. Discover how the platform you chose to use can incorporate drawing space, pictures, or web sites that you can use during your session. Offering these interactive tools are possible, it is just thinking outside the box.

A great resource to start with is the "American Telemedicine Associations Practice Guidelines for Telemental Health with Children and Adoles-

cence". [7]

[7] American Telemedicine Association Practice Guidelines for Telemental Health with Children and Adolescents. Telemed J E Health. 2017 10; 23(10):779-804.

Final Thoughts

As professionals we are taught "no harm done" and to always work within the scope of practice. Understanding the ethical, legal, and clinical implications of telehealth enhances our skill and commitment to the people we serve. Now that telehealth has finally hit the forefront of treatment we need to accept that it is much more than just "logging on" for our sessions.

While we know there are many similarities to the face to face skills we use, there are many differences we must understand. Patient safety as well as our own professional safety are of utmost importance when using this modality. You now have a greater understanding of the differences in the ethical, legal, and clinical spectrums.

Please continue with your education, knowledge,

and practice of telehealth treatment. We are only

starting to learn how beneficial it is when offering

services and treating our clients.

Resources

1. Informed Consent for Telehealth Services

2. Safety Check in Sheet

3. On-Line Resources

Informed Consent for Telehealth Services

The following information is provided to clients who are seeking Telehealth therapy. This document covers your rights, risks and benefits associated with receiving services, my policies, and your authorization. Please read this document carefully, note any questions you would like to discuss, and sign.

Telehealth Defined:

Telehealth means the remote delivering of health care services via technology-assisted media. This includes a wide array of clinical services and various forms of technology. The technology includes but is not limited to, a telephone, video, internet, a smartphone, tablet, PC desktop system or other electronic means. The delivery method must be secured by two-way encryption to be considered secure. Synchronous (at the same time) secure video chatting is the preferred method of service delivery. I use the HIPAA complaint, encrypted platform "Zoom" for all telehealth sessions.

Limitations of Telehealth Therapy Services:

While telehealth offers several advantages such as convenience and flexibility. It is an alternative form of therapy or adjunct to therapy and thus may involve disadvantages and limitations. For example, there may be a disruption to the service (e.g., phone gets cut off or video drops). This can be frustrating and interrupt the normal flow of personal interaction. Primarily, there is a risk of misunderstanding one another when communication lacks visual or auditory cues. For example, if video quality is lacking for some reason, I might not see various details such as facial expressions. Or, if audio quality is lacking, I might not hear differences in your tone of voice that I could easily pick up if you were in my office.

Additionally, the therapy office decreases the likelihood of interruptions. However, there are ways to minimize interruptions and maximize privacy and effectiveness. As the therapist, I will take every precaution to insure a technologically secure and environmentally private psychotherapy sessions. As the client, you are responsible for finding a private quite location where the sessions may be conducted. Consider using a "do not disturb" sign/note on the door. The virtual sessions must be conducted on a Wi-Fi connection for the best connection and to minimize disruption.

In Case of Technology Failure:

I understand that during a telehealth session we could encounter a technological failure. Difficulties with hardware, software, equipment, and/or services supplied by a 3rd party may result in service interruptions. If something occurs to prevent or disrupt any scheduled appointment due to technical complications and the session cannot be completed via online video conferencing, please call the therapist back at: XXX-XXX-XXXX. Please make sure you have a phone with you, and I have that phone number. We may also reschedule if there are problems with connectivity.

Structure and Cost of Sessions

I offer face-to-face psychotherapy when appropriate and available. However, based on your ability to make in-person sessions and my availability, I may provide virtual psychotherapy if your treatment needs determine that Telehealth services are appropriate for you. If appropriate, you may engage in either face-to-face sessions, Tele-health, or both. We will discuss what is best for you. Please remember that your insurance company may or may not cover therapy via phone or video. We are both responsible for understanding your mental health benefits. Please contact your insurance provider to verify coverage via Telehealth health.

The structure and cost of telehealth sessions are the same as face-to-face sessions described in my general "Client Contact and Insurance Information" form. Texting and emails (other than just setting up appointments) are billed at my hourly rate.

Payment Form, which will be sent to you separately if you have a financial responsibility for your session. I may charge your card without you being physically present. Your credit card will be charged at the conclusion of each Telehealth health interaction.

Email:

Email is not a secure means of communication and may compromise your confidentiality. However, I realize that many people prefer to email because it is a quick way to convey information. Nonetheless, please know that it is my policy to utilize this means of communication strictly for appointment confirmations. Please do not bring up any therapeutic content via email to prevent compromising your confidentiality. You also need to know that I am re-quired to keep a copy or summary of all emails as part of your clinical record that address anything related to ther-apy. I also strongly suggest that you only communicate through a device that you know is safe and technologically secure (e.g., has a firewall, anti-virus software installed, is password protected, not accessing the internet through a public wireless network, etc.). If you are in a crisis, please do not communicate this to me via email because I may not see it in a timely matter. Instead, please see below under "Emergency Management Plan".

Social Media - Facebook, Twitter, LinkedIn, Instagram, Pinterest, Etc.:

Please do not follow me on social media. It **will** compromise your confidentiality and blur the boundaries of our relationship. If this occurs, I will block you from social media sites. Please refrain from contacting me using social media messaging systems such as Facebook Messenger or Twitter. These methods have insufficient security, and I do not watch them closely. I would not want to miss an important message from you.

Electronic Transfer of PHI and Credit Card Transactions:

I utilize Payanywhere for billing and as the company that processes your credit card information. I may send the credit cardholder a text or an email receipt indicating that you used that credit card for my services, the date you used it, and the amount that was charged. This notification is usually set up two different ways - either upon your request at the time the card is run or automatically. Please know that it is your responsibility to know if you or the credit card-holder has the automatic receipt notification set up in order to maintain your confidentiality if you do not want a receipt sent via text or email. Additionally, please be aware that the transaction will appear on your credit card bill.

Cancellation Policy:

If you are unable to keep either a face-to-face appointment or a Telehealth appointment, you must notify me at least 24 hours in advance. If such advance notice is not received, you will be financially responsible for the no-show/cancellation rate of $50. Please note that insurance companies do not reimburse for missed sessions.

Emergency Management Plan

In the event of an emergency, it is imperative you are aware of resources in your area. As a precaution, please identify the primary residence where you anticipate being located for your telehealth session, the nearby emergency hospitals below. In addition, you will need to provide information for an emergency contact person. These all must be completed to participate in Telehealth health services.

1. Primary Address where you will be for telehealth Services:

____

____

Primary phone number: ____________________

2. Hospital Name and Location:

____

____

Hospital telephone number: ____________________

3. Emergency Contact Person:

____

____

Relationship: ____________________
Telephone Number: ____________________

You may alternatively follow this plan:

1. Call Lifeline at (800) 273-8255 (National Crisis Line)

2. Call 911.

3. Go to the emergency room of your choice.

I agree to take full responsibility for the security of any communications or treatment on my own computer or electronic device and in my own physical location.

I understand I am solely responsible for maintaining the strict confidentiality of my user ID, password, and/or connectivity link. I understand I am to use the ZOOM platform only at my scheduled session time. I understand it is not an avenue to contact **********. I shall not allow another person to use my user ID or connectivity link to access the services I also understand that I am responsible for using this technology in a secure and private location so that others cannot hear my conversation.

I understand that there will be no recording of any of the online session and that all information disclosed within sessions and the written records pertaining to those sessions are confidential and may not be revealed to anyone without my written permission, except where disclosure is required by law.

<u>**Consent to Treatment:**</u>

I voluntarily agree to receive online therapy services for an assessment, continued care, treatment, or other services and authorize ******** to provide such care, treatment, or services as are considered necessary and advisable. I understand and agree that I will participate in the planning of my care, treatment, or services and that I may withdraw consent for such care, treatment, or services that I receive through ******** at any time. By signing this Informed Consent, I, the undersigned client, acknowledge that I have both read and understood all the terms and information contained herein. Ample opportunity has been offered to me to ask questions and seek clarification of anything unclear to me.

Please know that I have the utmost respect and positive regard for you and your wellbeing. I would never do or say anything intentionally to hurt you in any way, and I strongly encourage you to let me know if something I have done or said has upset you. I always invite you to keep our communication open to reduce any possible harm. Please use technology with discretion. Only communicate limited information such as appointment request, cancellations, or estimated time of arrival.

I consent to the use of the following forms of communication via technology:

_____ Texting

_____ Email

_____ Fax

_____ Recommendations to Websites or Apps

Patient/Client Signature_________________________________

Parent, Guardian, or Legal Representative Signature (if minor or needed otherwise) _______________________________

Date ____________

My signature below indicates that I have discussed this form with you and have answered any questions you have regarding this information.

Clinician Signature ______________________________

Date ____________

Session Check in Sheet

1. Let others in your office/home space know you are entering a session.

    a. Have a specific person from your office identified to contact you via phone or by knocking on your door if an emergency occurs and you need assistance

2. Place a sign on your door stating, "Do not disturb in a telehealth session".

3. Silence your phone and turn off e-mail.

4. Make sure you can see a clock.

5. If you are going to share your screen or share from the EHR, open and make sure only your client's information is visible (minimize on screen).

<u>CONDUCTING THE SESSION</u>

1. Where are you today (address/location)? If we should get disconnected, what number should I use to reach you?

2. Is anyone else there with you?

    a. If no, begin session.

    b. If yes, who is there with you today?

3. Do you want to continue the session with ________ there with you?

    a. If no, end session.
    b. If yes, can we identify a word you can say to me that means to end the conversation "safe word"?

<u>ENDING THE SESSION</u>

1. Once the session is complete disconnect or "end" your meeting.

2. Take off and unplug headset.

3. Remove "Do not disturb" sign from your door.

4. Let others in your office space know you are off your telehealth session.

On-Line Resources

Organizations that have developed Ethical Codes and Standards:

www.EthicsCode.com (Guidelines for Mental Health and Healthcare Practice online)

www.ISMHO.org (International Society for Mental Health Online)

www.ihealthcoalition.org (Internet Healthcare Coalition)

www.ama-assn.org/ama (American Medical Association)
  Ethics – Industry Self-Regulation

- Guidelines for Mental Health and Healthcare Practice online
- International Society for Mental Health Online
- Internet Healthcare Coalition
- American Medical Association

Additional Information on State Regulations/Reimbursement
- http://www.telehealthresource-center.org/toolbox-module/cross-state-licensure
- Epstein, Becker, Green-50 State Survey of Telemental/Telebehavioral Health
- https://www.healthit.gov/providers-professionals/faqs/are-there-state-licensing-issues-related-telehealth

- https://www.zurinstitute.com/tele-health_across_state_lines-zur.html#overview
- http://cchpca.org/state-laws-and-reimburse-ment-policies
- http://www.ncsl.org/documents/health/tele-health2015.pdf

www.ingramcontent.com/pod-product-compliance
Lightning Source LLC
Chambersburg PA
CBHW061513250726
48657CB00005B/1832